Praise for 101 *Drama Games and Activities*

'I am a newly qualified teacher and always on the look out for resources that will help me in the studio and this book is perfect! The way in which the games are categorised into areas will save me time and also ensure that my warm ups etc are focused in the right direction and suited to the purpose of the lesson. The language used is straightforward and the instructions are easy to follow. I look forward to your next book.'

- Bernadette Collins, UK

'I am a newly certified theatre teacher and have to thank you for providing the most creative resources I have ever seen to educate and entertain young children.'

- Matt Brown, Milwaukee, USA

'This is a great resource, I am a student studying Primary school teaching - you helped with my final assessment! Thanks.'

- Felicity Ainsworth, Newcastle, NSW, Australia

'We wanted to congratulate you on a fantastic resource of ideas. Your games are perfect for our needs and we'll certainly be recommending your book to our staff. We hope that you are as excited as we are that some of your games could reach up to 12,000 children this year.'

- Fiona Hahn, King's Camps, Sheffield, UK

'As a Hebrew language and Judaic Studies teacher, I use a lot of drama in my classes. The students love it. Thank you for your awesome ideas. I am looking forward to using them in my next school year. I wish students all over will have a chance to play and enjoy your wonderful games.'

- Eran Rosenberg, Columbus, Ohio, USA

'I am a drama teacher and also work with young people outside of the curriculum. I now feel even better armed with ideas - having a Boal in one hand and your book in the other. Your book, like your web site is an amazing resource, which I am sure I will use frequently!'

- Sally Evans, Hull, UK

'I have just started teaching KS3 Drama in England. Am an NQT, had no drama training, and you've saved my sanity! '

- Jan Bishop, UK

'I am so thankful for your shared talent and free activity ideas. The kids will have a blast in a positive way as many of these activities will be added to our group. Thank You!!! Live Creative!'

- Jeanne, Tacoma, Washington, USA

'What a fantastic resource! Can't wait to get your book and share what you have compiled - it's great to know your games and exercises are tried and trusted and everything is explained extremely well. Thanks for sharing your passion!'

- Alison Howard, Adelaide, Australia

'I plan my lessons and try to remember the activities I have found in your book but I invariably have to refer to it (discretely) during my lessons. I never enter my drama lessons without it!'

- Janet Holroyd, Nice, France

'I have been looking for a book like this for years! I am so thrilled to finally find one! Thanks David for creating it. You should sell it in a book format at bookstores. It would sell amazingly!'

- Deborah Henry, Toronto, Canada

101

drama games
and activities

David Farmer

Second Edition

Disclaimer: All these games and exercises are undertaken entirely at your own risk and the author accepts no responsibility for any accident or injury sustained while using this book.

Further copies available from:
www.dramaresource.com
or www.lulu.com

Published by Lulu

ISBN 978-1-84753-841-3

About the author

After training as a primary school teacher, David Farmer worked in the theatre profession as a director, writer and actor. His plays have been performed across the USA, Canada, Ireland, Germany, Norway and throughout the United Kingdom. He composes music for many of his productions and is also a yoga teacher.

Since establishing Tiebreak Theatre Company in 1981, he has written, produced or performed in over 65 plays, reaching an audience of half a million young people. He has led hundreds of drama workshops with children, actors, students, teachers and prison inmates. He runs a popular drama website (www.dramaresource.com) and works freelance, based in Norwich, Norfolk.

Foreword

Drama games, bonding activities and improvisation can be daunting. Some people - children and adults - become inhibited by a fear of looking silly. Others feel they are expected to be funny and worry that they won't be. But David Farmer's helpful book offers activities that emphasize fun rather than embarrassment, and collaboration rather than self-exposure. I heartily recommend his techniques and ideas to all drama teachers and theatre directors.

David Wood OBE.
"...the National Children's Dramatist..." - The Times.

Introduction

This book contains a selection of drama games, activities and improvisation exercises which I have found to be effective in rehearsals and workshops with children and adults. I hope you find them useful in schools, colleges and universities, as well as in rehearsal rooms, management training courses and elsewhere. The activities will engender creativity and team spirit, whether working with children, actors, students, company directors or staff groups.

To help you find your way around, I have organised the games into categories. However many activities could easily fit into more than one category, so please experiment with them. These games were created for all kinds of reasons – that means you won't be breaking any rules if you want to adapt them according to your own needs. I have included some simple guidelines – but the most important is – have fun!

Some people will just want to play the games as an end in themselves, but you can also use them to lead into a themed lesson, or before and during rehearsal sessions.

My thanks are due to all the practitioners whose workshops I have attended, including Augusto Boal, Simon McBurney, Phelim McDermott, Roddy Maude-Roxby, Jon Oram, Toby Wilsher, Mike Wilson and John Wright. Thanks also to all the actors, teachers and children I have worked with, many of whom have taught me new games or inspired their creation.

David Farmer, April 2007.

Contents

Advice to the players

Structure each session to develop progressive awareness of:
- the body
- the body in space
- individual imaginative activity
- working with a partner
- working in a small group

And if you are working towards performance:
- being a performer
- being a member of the audience

- Begin with some simple stretches, so that individuals become more aware of their own bodies.

- Continue with activities that bring awareness of the space – such as Space walk.

- It is easy for the group to become deeply involved in imaginative activity, so you will need to establish a clear method of control, letting them know when to stop and listen. For example, everyone practices being completely still when you raise your arm, or when you say "Freeze!" Alternatively you could use a small bell or tambourine to call attention, or have a cushion or chair that you sit on when it is time to meet together.

- Establish clear routines, such as sitting down when the group enters the room and circle time at the end.

- Concentration exercises can be particularly useful for groups beginning drama.

- At some point you may want to warm up the voice including some tongue twisters.

- If work is being shown, encourage each group to give positive comments about other presentations. This helps to improve attention while groups wait to show their work.

- Physical games and activities are a refreshing way to harness creativity, opening up new avenues to lateral thinking.

- Warm-up games can be a great way to start rehearsals. Keep the focus with group dynamic and concentration games.

- Drama games help make rehearsal periods more creative for the whole company and can often lead to new ideas for staging a scene.

- Drama can be used as a tool in many subject areas, for example history, creative writing and story telling, enabling students to find new ways to explore ideas.

- At the end, find time to discuss the session, perhaps finishing with a relaxing visualisation exercise, such as Desert Island.

- Enjoy the games and activities - I hope you find them useful!

Icebreakers

These games can be effective in many situations, providing a novel way to begin group activities and for people to begin to get to know each other.

Catch my name
A fun way of learning names. The group stands in a circle and begins by throwing a beanbag or bouncing a medium-sized ball, such as a children's football, across the circle from one person to another. Make sure people are ready to throw and ready to catch. Eye contact is important. Now, introduce yourself as you throw or bounce the ball across the circle – "Hi, I'm David". Once everybody has had a go at that, continue the game but this time say the name of the person that you are throwing to – "Jessica to Kelvin". The group should ensure that everybody receives the ball. One way of doing this is for everybody to hold one hand up until they have caught the ball, or each person folds their arms when they have thrown it.

- As a variation, the catcher can call out the name of the thrower.
- Ask everybody to call out the name of the thrower.
- More balls can be added in so that it develops into a *Group juggle*.
- Don't make name games into an actual test – people are less likely to learn names if they feel pressurised. Keep it light and enjoyable.
- A useful adaptation for language learners – use word categories so that each person throwing the ball must say a word in the named category.

Name show

A fun way of learning names. Stand in a circle. Everyone must imagine that they are the host of a Game Show. One person at a time introduces themselves proudly to the rest of the group with a "signature" by saying (or even singing) their name and making an action to go with it. Everybody else then copies the name and movement. When you have gone right round the circle you can develop the game a step further. One person starts off by making someone else's signature. That person must now choose another person in the group and make their signature, and so on.

Nutty names

Going round a circle, people introduce themselves by adding a word beginning with the same letter as their first name, for example, "Peculiar Pete", "Jumping Josephine" or "Sorted Sid". They could also add an action.

- To help remember the names, you could pass a ball around the circle with each person saying the nutty name of the person they are throwing to.
- Or, you could go round twice and the second time they must say the name and do the action of the person on their left.
- Even the simplest name games do help you to remember names – it has been scientifically proven.

Three changes

A getting to know you exercise. Two partners sit back to back and change three details of their appearance, for example the way they wear their hair, how their blouse is buttoned, which wrist they wear their watch on. They turn back and each has to try and spot the changes made.

Heels and toes

A fun introductory warm up game, good for breaking the ice with a new group. First, you need to practice the technique on your own: Stand with your heels together and your toes facing outwards in a 'V' shape. Place your hands in front of you with the palms facing the floor. Bring the heels of your hands together and the tips of your fingers away from each other so that you make another V shape. Now jump up in the air and reverse the shape made by your hands and feet. When you land back on the floor, your big toes should be touching, with the heels apart, and the index finger tips should be connected to each other, with the wrists apart. Try jumping a few times, reversing the shape each time.

That was the easy part. Now comes the proper part of the game. Start again with the V shape made by your feet (heels together, toes apart), but make the *opposite* shape with your hands (index finger tips together, wrists apart). Try jumping in the air and reversing both shapes before you land. This seems nigh impossible – but comes with practice. You will find that your brain keeps trying to get your hands and feet to make corresponding shapes. When (if) you get really quite good at it, teach the whole manoeuvre to a group. They will be very impressed and find the whole thing a hilarious challenge. Great for encouraging a serious group to relax with each other.

Two truths, one lie

Highly recommended for getting to know each other in a new group. Tell your partner three things about yourself – two of which are true and one of which is a lie. Now introduce your partner to the rest of the group and see if they can guess which was the lie.

Alternatively, tell your partner three true things about yourself and then swap over. Now the whole group makes a circle. Each partner introduces their friend to the group – they tell the group two of the true things and make up one lie about their partner.

Greetings

Players mill around the space. On a given signal, they greet the next person they meet, then continue walking. The leader calls out a new way of greeting each time. Examples could be:

- Greet a long-lost friend
- Greet shyly
- Greet a famous person
- Greet someone you know a secret about
- Greet under water
- Greet someone on the ledge of a high mountain
- Greet as an Eskimo (rub noses)
- Greet as a Martian (make it up)

Getting into groups

It can sometimes be hard to break the class into smaller groups without somebody being left over, or the same people always working with each other – so why not make it into a game? Call out a number, and people have to get into groups of that number. If they don't have enough in their group, they should make it look like there are the right number of people by spreading themselves out – making the group look bigger! The number can be as big or small as you like. Towards the end, pick a number that is the size of the group you want for the next exercise. Hopefully they will be fairly mixed up by then!

Half-a-minute handshake

A quick warm up and getting to know you game. Everyone in the room must shake hands with, say "hello" and their name to everybody else within thirty seconds.

As a variation, give a signal for the class to switch between normal and slow motion movement and speech and back again.

See also:

Clap around the circle
Cross the circle
Fruit salad
Human knot
One-two-three
Slap clap click click

Warm ups

Warm ups are a great way of bridging the gap into rehearsals or into a drama session, encouraging participants to "let their hair down" a bit, to move their bodies and use their voices, to work with a partner or as a member of a group.

Space walk
This game is invaluable for the development of group and spatial awareness.

- "Find a space to stand in. When I clap my hands, walk quietly around the room in any direction. Try to fill the space - move into empty areas. Keep changing direction. Try not to come into contact with other people. Now Freeze!"

Check that everyone stands absolutely still, freezing every muscle. Ask them to notice areas of the room which are emptier. Repeat the exercise with any of the following variations:

- Avoid eye contact.
- Make eye contact with every person you pass.
- Every now and again, shake hands with someone and move on.
- Find a new way of moving in the space. And another way, low down. And another, high up.
- On a signal, move in slow motion, then normal, then fast, all the time being aware of other people.
- Imagine you are moving through thick snow, over ice, under water, on hot sand, through an art gallery…
- Freeze!
- Play *Noses*

- Make physical contact with one other person and continue moving together in the space. Find new ways of moving together.
- Move apart from your partner but maintain eye contact, without bumping into anyone else.
- And freeze again. Notice exactly where you are in relation to others around you. Run and touch each of the four walls and return to exactly the same place without bumping into anyone.

Bomb and shield

Without letting anybody else know, each person must choose two other people in the room. Tell them that the first person they chose is a bomb and the second person is a shield. On a signal everybody starts moving around the room with the aim of staying as far away from the bomb as possible and keeping the shield between him or her and the bomb! You can give a signal to freeze at any moment to check whether they are doing it correctly. The group will probably end up spread out, so as a contrast, you could also play *Noses*.

Yes, let's!

Whole group game. One person starts with a suggested action - "Let's play the piano", for example. Everyone else shouts, "Yes, let's!" and the whole group carries out the action with as much enthusiasm as possible. After a while someone else can suggest a new action - "Let's be spies!" - "Yes, let's!" The aim is for the whole group to fully commit to the activity. Try not to rush too quickly from one activity to the next - explore each one for a while. A good warm-up for impro work.

Group juggle

There are several variations of this game. A ball is thrown across the circle from one person to the next. Once the action is going smoothly, a second ball is introduced, perhaps of a different size or colour. This one could be bounced or thrown across the circle. You can continue adding as many balls as the group can manage.

It is important to maintain focus and to stop and start again if the game gets out of control. As ever, communication is essential – just as it is between actors on stage. Make sure you have eye contact *before* you throw. Group members should aim to take responsibility for each another.

- In one variation a single ball is thrown so that everyone catches it once. Then the group tries to repeat exactly the same pattern – but faster and faster – without making a mistake. Add in more balls one by one, to be thrown in the same order.

- Try also having one person stand in the middle of the circle. The job of the people around the circle is to throw the ball to that person, who must then throw it to somebody else. No-one should ever throw the ball until they know the person in the middle is ready. Again, more balls can be introduced.

- For adults – if somebody drops the ball, they say "Oh, balls". The game starts again when everybody is focussed. This takes the edge off making a mistake.

- An amusing twist on the game is to use all sorts of objects instead of, or as well as balls – rubber chickens, cuddly toys and beanie babies.

Clap the ball

Begin by throwing a tennis ball or beanbag to each other across a circle. The person throwing the ball has responsibility for whether the other person catches it – so make sure that people are clear about whom they are throwing to. Once this is working well, introduce the idea that everyone must clap their hands in unison once, while the ball is in the air. Complicity between group members is essential.

If this goes well, the game continues so that each time the ball is thrown, the group try to clap together one extra time. So the first time it is thrown, everyone claps once, the second time twice, and so on. You will probably get up to seven or eight and then it will start to get more difficult. Once it breaks down, start again from one. This is an effective way of encouraging concentration and awareness.

Stick in the mud

A children's playground version of tag which can be played by children or fit adults as a warm-up. One person is chosen to be "it" and has to try and get everybody else stuck in the mud. The others have to avoid being caught by running away. If the person who is "it" manages to tag (touch) them, that person stays where they are with their arms outstretched and their legs wide apart. Anyone else who has not yet been caught can try to release others who are stuck in the mud. They do this by diving or crawling through their legs. If they manage to get through without being caught, then both people can run away. It is quite hard to catch everybody, but a good (and energetic) catcher can do it by guarding those who are already caught.

Fruit salad

A game that is easier to play than to explain - and great fun! Everyone thinks of the name of a type of fruit. The object is to say the name of somebody else's fruit three times before they can say the name of yours. Before you begin, go round the circle with everybody naming their fruit – they must all be different.

Person **A** steps into the middle of the circle. Let's assume their chosen fruit is "apricot". **A** then has to try and say the name of one of the other fruits (e.g. "kiwi") three times really quickly. Whoever chose kiwi as their fruit (person **B**) has to start saying "apricot apricot apricot" straight away. However if **A** manages to say "kiwi" three times before **B** starts saying "apricot, apricot, apricot" then **B** has to be in the middle and **A** joins the circle again. **B** then has to say the name of anybody else's fruit three times and can only be stopped by that person saying the name of **B**'s fruit. When people get good at this, it is quite difficult for the person in the middle to get out again. They have to keep trying to say the name of different people's fruit until they catch someone out.

Kitty in the corner

This is a classic children's game. Four players sit on chairs at the corners of the playing area, with one player (Kitty) in the middle. Two people at any of the corners try to swap places by making eye contact with each other and then moving as quickly as possible, before Kitty can capture one of the corners. Whoever doesn't manage to sit down becomes (or remains) Kitty in the middle. You are not allowed to return to your seat once you have left it. With a larger group you can make a circle of chairs. However, you should ensure eye contact is used clearly to avoid collisions.

Keepy-uppy

A fun warm-up game for re-energising people first thing in the morning or after lunch. You need a room with a high ceiling, or you could play it outside if it is not too windy. You also need a ball – I like to use a children's football. One person begins by hitting or throwing the ball as high into the air as possible. Members of the group try and stop the ball from hitting the ground by hitting it with any part of the body. Nobody is allowed to hit the ball twice in succession.

At first, the game can appear to be quite difficult. After a while you can point out that the way to play the game is to work together. Everybody must take responsibility for the ball remaining in the air. If someone is about to drop it, help them out. Try to be aware of who you are hitting the ball to next. Keep it high. It is good to set a target and then increase it – keep the ball in the air for twenty hits, then thirty, then fifty. The group will become quite motivated towards achieving the target (in fact it may be hard to stop them from playing!).

- Although you can use any part of the body, it is best to start off by just using the hands - using feet can lead to loss of control.
- If you are playing indoors you can allow people to bounce the ball off the wall (depending on light-fittings and windows!).
- A challenging variation is that every fifth hit should be with a part of the body that is not the hands.
- People will become more skilful the more they play the game.

Bill and Ben

You need to know the *original* tune of the famous BBC children's television programme to play this rather silly game. (Listen to it at http://www.david-farmer.com/bab.htm.) Everyone stands in a circle. First of all, sing the song as a group. The words are not too complicated:

Bill and Ben, Bill and Ben,
Bill and Ben, Bill and Ben,
Flowerpot Men.

When everyone is confident of the tune, the game begins. One person starts by singing the first word from the song. The person on their left sings the next word, and so on – a little like telling a one word at a time story. Try to keep the tempo smooth. "Flowerpot" can be sung as one or two words – it's up to you!

Once this has been mastered, the next rule is that the person singing "Bill" must bend their knees at the same time as singing the word – just that person. When that is working, add the next rule – *everybody* bends their knees when *anyone* sings "Ben". This usually results in much laughter, with people bending their knees at the wrong times. If you lose the flow of the tune, start again.

Sword and shield

In pairs, each holds one open hand against his or her own back, palm facing outwards. The index finger of the other hand is held out in front like a sword; each tries to stab their partner's "shield". Score a point for each strike. Five points and you're out!

Sound and action

In a circle, the first person makes any kind of simultaneous sound and action. Following this, everybody else tries to copy the sound and movement as exactly as possible, at the same time. The next person along makes a new sound and action, which everybody copies. It's best if you try to come up with the sound and action on the spur of the moment rather than preplanning it.

The game should move quite quickly. This is a fun warm-up, and it is usually possible to go around the circle a couple of times without losing interest. It is liberating to see everyone else copy your own sound and action. Encourage the group to explore different ways of moving, including different heights.

- One variation is that the first person makes their sound and action to their neighbour, who copies it, turns to the next person and makes a completely different sound and action. This continues round the group.
- A concentration game can be played in this way: Go round the circle once with everybody making up his or her own unique sound and action. Then one person makes her own sound and action once, followed by the sound and action made by any other person. That person makes his or her sound and action followed by somebody else's – and so on. See how long you can keep it going.
- An ideal follow-up activity would be to use the sounds and action which have been created to make an abstract machine in the centre of the circle, with everybody finding a way to add in their own repeating sound and action in relation to the others. At the end you could decide what kind of machine it was.

Giving presents
A fast-moving game in which ideas are generated very quickly. In pairs, mime giving and receiving presents. The person giving the present must not decide what it is. The recipient should mime opening the present and only then say what it is. *Don't pre-plan, just decide on the spur of the moment. Whatever it is, be really delighted and grateful – it is just what you have always wanted!* Then quickly swap over and give a present back. Keep swapping over for a few minutes.

- Afterwards it is fun to go around the circle and find out some of the presents people received.
- Try playing an even faster version where the gift is not wrapped so that the recipient immediately says what it is and thanks the giver.

What are you doing?
Stand in a circle. The first person (A) starts miming an activity, such as eating an apple. The person to their left (B) says "What are you doing?". A keeps miming and at the same time says the name of a different activity. For example, if A was miming eating an apple, they could say "playing the piano". B then starts playing a piano. A stops their mime. Now the third person (C) asks B , "What are you doing?". B keeps playing the piano and names a different activity, which C must mime. And so it goes on.

There should be no repetition and no similar activities. For example if you are miming climbing a ladder you cannot say, "climbing the stairs". Equally you should not name an activity that looks like the one you are actually doing. For example, if you are cleaning a window you cannot say "waving good-bye" - because it looks very similar!

20

Ten second objects

In small groups. The name of an object is called out and the group has to make the shape of that object out of their own body shapes, while the leader counts down slowly from ten to zero. Usually every group will find a different way of forming the object. Examples could be:

- A car
- A ship
- A washing machine
- A fire
- A clock

- You could choose objects from a play you are rehearsing or a theme you are exploring.
- Groups can also be given a few minutes to devise two objects of their own which the rest of the class try to guess.
- You could make it a rule that after 10 seconds they must be completely frozen in position.
- On the other hand it can be fun if they are able to make objects that use movement.

Traffic lights

A physical warm-up game. The leader calls out traffic light colours in any order, trying to catch people out.

- "Green" - Walk/run around the space.
- "Amber" - Stand on one leg without over-balancing.
- "Red" - Stop still - or lie down on the ground!

Zip zap boing

Concentration and warm-up game in a circle. A sport played with an imaginary frisbee. One person starts by passing the frisbee to their right or left, saying "zip!". The next person catches it and passes it on with a "zip!" When everybody has had a go, "boing!" is introduced. Anyone may now change the direction of travel by raising their hands as though deflecting the "frisbee" and saying "boing!". It is then passed back the other way with a "zip!" Finally, "zap!" is introduced. Here, anyone may pass the "frisbee" across the circle with a "zap!" Eye contact is essential throughout. People may "boing!" back and forth to one another (as long as they don't go on for too long). Make sure people don't say "zip" when they mean "zap"!

See also:

Follow your nose
Guess the leader
Half-a-minute handshake
Grandma's footsteps
Getting into groups
Mirror movers
Noses
One-two-three
Slap clap click click
Walking breath

Improvisation

These exercises can help to introduce many of the skills required for the group to create their own scenes and plays by focussing on the development of situations, characters and status relationships. The activities cover improvised speech and action, the use of props, an understanding of physical theatre, subtext, devising and directing.

Yes, and...
It's really important to accept each other's ideas in drama. Here is a game played with a partner to help you do just that. One person begins by making an "offer" (putting forward an idea) and the partner replies with a sentence that begins "Yes, and...". Try not to block your partner's ideas, which can so often happen in improvisation. Instead, try and build on each other's suggestions. As soon as confidence develops, you can add in actions.

A: It's raining
B: Yes, and I've got a large umbrella
A: Let's shelter under it
B: Yes, and the wind is blowing us into the air
A: We are flying over the sea
B: Yes, and we have landed on an island...

And so on. It can be a very liberating game, especially as we don't often get the chance to say "yes" to everything! Participants should avoid trying to push their own idea at the expense of their partner's. Use the space as much as possible. Afterwards you can tell your adventure to the rest of the group. You could also try the game with both of you saying "Yes, and...". The literal "Yes" can be dropped completely as soon as acceptance of each others' ideas begins to become more automatic.

Alphabet conversation

Have a conversation where each sentence begins with the next letter of the alphabet. This may seem difficult at first, but improves with practice. It's a good idea to set a situation before you begin. You can also use sounds to start a sentence, for example "Mmmm" or "tut-tut". Can be played in pairs or small groups. Here is an example:

A: Anyone seen my cat?
B: Black one, with funny eyes?
A: Can't say I remember.
B: Don't tell me you've forgotten what it looks like?
A: Every cat looks the same to me.
B: Fortunately, I found one yesterday
A: Gee, that's great...

- You could also try starting somewhere in the middle of the alphabet. Then when you reach "Z", return to "A" until you arrive back where you started.
- You can combine this technique with *One word stories*.

Spin-offs

Two people hold hands and start spinning around. On a given signal, they let go and spin away from each other, ending in any random position. It doesn't matter if they fall down on the floor or are still standing up. Immediately they start an improvisation suggested to them by the position they have ended up in – it can be abstract or naturalistic. If necessary, you can decide beforehand which partner will begin speaking, although eventually they should be able to play the game without this help. Try to find a way to end the scene.

Status pictures

In pairs, create a still image where one of you has a higher status than the other. Show your image to the others and let them guess who is "high" and who is "low". Discuss why there may be areas of disagreement. Make another image showing high and low status in a different way. Try to make an image where you have equal status and see if the onlookers agree!

Pecking order

In groups of three, decide on a situation and three characters, e.g. a surgery, with a doctor, nurse and patient. One person leaves the room and the others decide on their own pecking order or status - 1, 2 or 3. They also decide what status the other person is (without telling them). The person re-enters and the improvisation begins. After a while, the improvisation is stopped and the third person has to guess their own status and that of the other two.

You can make the game more challenging by having two people with the same status. It is most fun if you steer away from the obvious pecking order, e.g. the patient can be 1, the nurse 2 and the doctor 3.

Example characters:
- Detective and two suspects
- Boss, secretary and interviewee
- Television director, scriptwriter and actor.

Make friends/argue

In pairs, walk around the room, making friends. Now when the leader tells you, find something to argue about - then make friends again. Keep swapping between making friends and having an argument. Try to continue the conversation, whatever happens.

Shoe shuffle

Pass any easy-to-handle object around the circle – or place it in the centre – for example a shoe, a bucket or a chair. Each person uses it in turn - changing it into a different object each time. It can be anything - apart from what it really is.

- As a variation, other members of the group can step into the improvisation so that a short scene develops.
- Try doing it to music.

Round robin

Two people start an improvisation (with or without speech). A third person enters, changing the situation in some way and one of the original pair finds an excuse to leave.

In another variation, the two people continue their improvisation until somebody in the group shouts, "Freeze!" Both actors freeze and whoever asked them to stop taps one of them on the shoulder, replacing that person and taking up exactly the same pose. The new person starts a different improvisation linked to the position both players are in.

Talk to me like the rain
The group stand in a circle. They are given the following two-line dialogue:

A: Talk to me like the rain.
B: Much ado about nothing.

One person chooses someone across the circle, crosses over to him or her and says "Talk to me like the rain". That person replies, "Much ado about nothing". The first person steps into their place and the second now crosses to a third, with the same two-line dialogue taking place. The aim is to put different emphases on the words each time - to find different ways of playing the lines. Players can be given different emotions to express through the lines or they can just come up with their own way each time. There are usually quite a wide variety of scenes. You could use two lines from a play you are rehearsing or any lines that you want to make up.

Hands through
An absurd impro exercise. Person **A** stands behind person **B** and puts her arms underneath B's arms so that they protrude in front. At the same time, **B** clasps his hands behind his own back. Now any scene is improvised but **A** moves her arms as though they were the arms of person **B**. You could, for example, ask **B** to give some kind of lecture, but **A** would provide all the gestures! Or, you could have two "hands-through" pairs facing each other as though they were meeting each other. Of course, in theory, **A** can do anything she likes to **B** – scratching his head, stroking his chin, waving furiously, drinking a glass of water and so on.

Breakfast serial

This exercise helps to introduce the concept of subtext in a fun way. In pairs or small groups of three or four, improvise a short naturalistic scene where people are having breakfast together. Each person should speak two or three lines each. For example:

A: Good morning.
B: Morning.
A: Please pass me the milk.
B: I'm afraid we've run out.
A: Has the paper come?
B: It's right in front of you.

Nothing dramatic needs to happen. Now repeat the scene a couple of times, until you remember the words exactly. Some or all of the groups could show their scenes to the rest. Each pair has now created a short "script".

Give a new situation, for example, spies meeting at a secret rendezvous, two detectives grilling a suspect or staff in an operating theatre. Each pair is given a few minutes to improvise the new scenario – but must find a way to use the exact lines from the breakfast scene. Put as much activity into the scene as you can. Suddenly a simple everyday conversation becomes imbued with new meaning!

- There can be sections of the scene where no talking takes place.
- Try to make sense of every word in your script – even if it seems impossible at first!
- Each group could choose their own new situation.
- Subtext includes the action in a scene and characters' real thoughts and motives.

Blank characters

In pairs, partner **A** thinks of a real situation that has occurred in his life, involving a disagreement between himself and another person. Partner **B** is a "blank" character and is told nothing about the situation. **A** begins to play the situation, using **B** as the other character - but communicating only with facial expressions. It is a good idea if both characters are sitting down at this point. **B** responds back, using only facial expression.

On a signal, **A** uses his body to communicate as well - but without moving from the spot. Next he uses his body in the space, moving around. Each time **B** responds, using the same style of communication as **A**. The next stage is the addition of gibberish - speaking in any made up sounds that come to mind. Finally **A** uses face, body, space and real words to communicate. Afterwards, discuss how much of the situation **B** guessed before speech was used.

Future perfect

In groups, make up a very short scene or still image, summarising a topical environmental, social or political problem. Show your image/scene to the others. Now devise a second scene to show the ideal solution to the problem. Discuss whether the second situation is realistically achievable.

Martian and earthling

In pairs, one is the Martian and the other the Earthling. The Martian chooses an everyday object and imagines they have found it, but don't know what it is used for. They describe its shape, texture, colour, weight etc to the Earthling, who can ask any questions (apart from its name!), and must guess what it is. To make it harder, both partners should sit on their hands.

Experts
In pairs, one is a TV interviewer, the other is an "expert" on any subject the interviewer names - e.g. abstract art, eating jelly, catching caterpillars... Now an interview takes place and the expert must talk as though he or she really knows a lot about the subject.

As a fun variation in threes, the expert speaks gibberish (any made up sounds) and an "interpreter" explains what the expert is really saying. In this case, you could try not giving a theme before you start, so that the interpreter can say whatever she likes! Of course it is essential that both the expert and the interpreter go along with each other's ideas.

You can also use the one word at a time technique and allow this game to get very silly! You could have two people playing the interviewer and another pair as the expert. To give a bit more control, you could try one interviewer and a two-headed expert.

It would be best to get some practice in this technique first - see *One Word Stories*.

Who am I?
Played by the whole class or a large group. One person leaves the room. The others choose where the improvisation takes place and who the player will be. Ideally the character should be one who is surrounded by a lot of activity; for example a newsreader in a studio or news room, an Inspector at a police station, a porter in a factory. The activity begins and the first player is asked to return. The other players should relate to the first player and try to include him in what is happening. It is important that the focus is on an improvisation rather than a guessing game. The first player should be open to what happens and not try to rush the discovery.

People poems

Divide into small groups of around four or five. Each group is given a word - e.g. "Time". Each person writes down or remembers two or three words associated with the theme, e.g. slow, fast, boredom, quickly, centuries. Now the group has to make an object out of the members, linked to the theme (such as a clock). Ideally the object should move. Next the group brings the object to life and works out a way of bringing in some or all of their words - linked to their movements. They show the resulting People Poem to the rest of the class, who can try and guess the theme.

Themes could include:
- Elements - earth, air, fire, water
- Opposites – cold/hot, fast/slow, high/low
- Colours
- Emotions

Physical theatre

Try combining two drama techniques to create an original physical theatre piece: For example, play *Ten second objects* with a seasonal flavour - ask the groups to make a bonfire and different kinds of fireworks (with appropriate sounds and slow-motion movement). Once they have tried out a few ideas, bring in your second technique – *still images*. Each group has to create a series of three frozen images showing different scenes, which could take place on bonfire night (or whatever your theme is). They could also decide on a caption for each image. Get the groups to show their series of images to each other.

Finally ask them to devise a short scene which begins with an object made out of their bodies, which slowly metamorphoses into a scene based on one or more of their frozen images - and perhaps at the end of the scene they become a second object. This is a simple way of creating some effective physical theatre.

Scene from your life

A good exercise for learning about directing, or for getting to know one another. Divide into small groups. One member of the group tells the others a true story of an event from her life. It should involve the same number of people as there are in the group (excluding the teller of the story, who becomes the director). The director chooses members of the group to play the various characters involved, including herself. Once the actors are sure of the story, they improvise it from beginning to end. The director gives them notes and they improvise it again, trying to make it as true as possible.

You can take time to develop short sections of the story if the director feels they are not accurate enough. It's a great experience being the director, because you know exactly what you want the actors to do. It's also fun for the actors as they feel quite responsible for getting the story right and finding the "inner truth" of the characters - especially the person who plays the role of the protagonist. This exercise involves many of the skills involved in putting on a play: choosing a story, deciding how it should be told, casting, acting, directing and devising.

As an adaptation, begin by asking the group to decide on three strong *still images* from the story. These can be shown to the other groups just before each group devises and rehearses their performance. If they try to include the images within their scene it will help to make it more physically dynamic.

See also:

Free association mime
Game of power
Gibberish
Moulding a character
Random sound story
Three moments

Mime and movement

These activities develop physical awareness and bodily expression. They can help to enhance performances by introducing physical theatre techniques. For those who don't enjoy spoken improvisation, the games may open up a multitude of other possibilities in drama – and mime and movement are essential skills for any actor.

Follow the hand

In pairs, "A" holds her hand palm outwards a few inches away from her partner's face. Now she moves her hand slowly and "B" tries to keep his face the same distance away, moving his body wherever needed. As a variation, try both leading the other (slowly!), or in threes, each leading another whilst being led themselves!

Follow your nose

A movement exercise for the whole group. Move around the room, filling up the space, changing pace, changing direction, being aware of other people but not touching them. Now become aware of your nose. Let your nose lead you around the room. Follow it wherever it goes!

Develop this by focussing on different parts of the body, so that participants begin to discover new ways of moving. Very useful for dance or physical theatre, or simply for discovering movement ideas for characters. Try being led by your stomach, your little toe, your knee, your back and so on.

Complete the image

In front of the class, two people shake hands. Freeze the image at any moment. Ask the group what meaning this image might have. Where could the people be - and what might they be doing? One partner removes herself, leaving the other frozen. She looks at the remaining half-image and decides what it could represent. She adds herself back into the picture in a different pose, completing the image to show a new meaning. The other partner unfreezes, looks at the image and completes it afresh.

Now try it in pairs. Begin by shaking hands and then freezing in position. Continue by stepping in and out of the image. Encourage players to "think with their bodies" - it is more important to work quickly rather than think too literally.

Free association mime

A variant on *Yes and*. Work with a partner. Person **A** begins miming an activity or situation. **B** must join in somehow. He could mime being in the same situation or carrying out a similar or related activity. At some point **B** should change the activity or situation. Then **A** must change her activity so that the ideas swap and change between them. For example **A** mimes eating a banana. **B** also eats a banana and becomes a monkey in the zoo. **A** becomes a child looking in the cage. The two react to each other. Then **B** decides he is a doctor and **A** is his patient... and so on.

- Make sure you accept your partner's idea and then develop or change it.
- You can be as free ranging and imaginative with your ideas as you like.

Crossing the line
In pairs - hold your arms straight out in front and place your palms against your partner's hands with the fingers pointing upwards. On a signal both people start pushing, trying to move their partner backwards (this part should not go on for very long!).

Repeat the exercise, but this time ask the partners to purposely play so that one partner is winning for a while and then the other, with the leadership swapping a few times. Next, the two partners step apart so that there is a six-inch gap between their hands. Once again they repeat the exercise, trying to make it look real, but keeping the gap the whole time. This can be challenging, as it is tempting to keep trying to win!

You may notice that people who find it difficult to "lose" this game are probably the same people that find it difficult to play low-status in improvisation. This can be a good introduction to discussing status work. You could usefully follow this exercise with *Status pictures*.

The exercise is not so much about pushing your partner over a line, but crossing the line from reality to imagination!

Mirrors
Two people stand facing each other and one tries to reflect the other's movements as accurately as possible. Make sure movements are slow and smooth. On a given signal, the leading swaps over.

- Keep the flow of movement each time there is a changeover.
- If you get really tuned into each other, you may find that neither person is leading!

Mirror movers

Three or more actors stand in a triangle configuration, facing in one direction. The person in front begins a movement, which the other two copy smoothly. If the group turns so that somebody else is in front, then that person takes over leading the movements. After a while, the group can increase tempo and change leaders quickly. Then introduce travel - the group can move around the space, trying to keep the same distance between each other.

- This could be developed as a method of creating choreography for a crowd scene.

Mime whispers

Each person chooses an everyday task, such as making a cup of tea, washing-up, writing a letter, drawing a picture and so on. Everyone practices miming that activity on their own – broken down into exactly six movements. It's important that this is practiced so it can be remembered later.

- In pairs, show each other the mime you were doing, without talking or explaining. Show the mime once only.
- Everybody move on to find a new partner.
- Try to show your partner the last mime you observed – of course it will not be easy.

Again the partners separate and move on to find yet new partners. After three or four swaps, it is time to observe the results. Individuals are asked to show the final mime they observed. The teacher can then ask if anyone recognises it as their own original mime. If they do, they can show the original mime alongside the final version. Some of the mimes may stay fairly intact, while others will be unrecognisable!

Group shape

The aim is to make one abstract shape out of the whole group. One person goes into the centre of the circle and makes a shape with his body. Another person finds a way of adding herself into the existing shape in any way she likes. One at a time, the rest of the group come into the circle and become part of the group shape. Ask people to think about how their shape complements or contrasts with existing shapes. Encourage the use of different levels – low, medium and high. If you have a camera, it is often worth taking a photo of the finished shape.

Now ask everyone to become aware of exactly where they are in relation to everybody else, which parts of their body are in contact with other people or with the floor and how they are balanced. Everybody returns to their places around the circle. On a given signal every person moves in slow motion into the space at the same time to recreate the group shape as exactly as possible. Once the shape has been recreated ask if people feel that they are in *exactly* the same place as before. It is rare that they do.

This exercise is good practice for crowd scenes or ensemble work. It encourages an awareness of movement, balance and physical relationships with other people. You could use it to develop an interesting beginning to any crowd scene.

Points of contact

Make an interesting shape with your body where you have two points of contact with the floor (it could be just standing). Find a new way of making two points of contact with the floor – and another way. Move about, always keeping two parts of the body in contact with the floor. Try again with three points. The points of contact could be anything – a foot, an elbow, fingers, knee, head etc.

Now make a shape with a partner – having a certain number of points of contact with the floor – try 3, 5, 12 and so on. Finally you can do the same thing in small groups. The exercise makes you more aware of your contact with the floor and how you balance, as well as encouraging you to use your body more creatively on your own and with others.

Throw your face
The group stands in a circle. The first person puts their hands over their face and moves them about as though sculpting their own features. *Move your lips, tongue, eyes, eyebrows - anything that you can move - into a grotesque face. When you are ready take your hands away to show your face to the group!*

Choose somebody across the circle. Lean backwards and then quickly forwards as though you are throwing your face to them. Now comes the really funny part - that person must quickly copy the face you made as though they have "caught" it. This is usually quite amusing for everybody else as well.

That person moulds a new expression with their hands and throws it across the circle to somebody new - and so the game goes on!

Animal animation
Sit in a space on your own. Decide on an animal. Imagine yourself as that animal, asleep in its home. Begin to wake up and sense the world around you. Move around slowly to explore your immediate environment. After a while you find food. Suddenly you sense danger. Luckily you escape just in time and go back to your home. Out of role, discuss with the group what kind of danger you faced.

Essence machines

This technique is useful for generating physical and aural ideas around a theme. A topic is chosen and people are asked to think of a repeating sound and action linked to that theme. One person starts off in the centre of a circle with their own sound and movement, then one by one the others step in, finding a suitable way to add in their own ideas. The machine can be frozen, then played back at twice or half the "normal" speed. Themes could include: optimism, pessimism, supermarket; hospital; bullying; emotions. You could have a machine that actually makes something, like chocolate biscuits, school dinners or weather conditions.

Carbon copies

Choose a theme, for example, "emotions". Without talking, the group sculpts one person into a given position, e.g. "surprise". When the sculpture is finished, all the others copy the shape with their own bodies, as exactly as possible. The "sculpture" now unfreezes and looks at the other participants. Someone else is sculpted with a different emotion or idea – e.g. "fear". When enough people have had a turn, the group could use the shapes they have invented to make a group picture on the theme, linking different shapes or statues together to make a scene or abstract image.

See also:

Guess the leader
Moulding a character
People poems
Random images
Shoe shuffle
Space walk
Status pictures
Ten second objects
Three moments
Walk together
What are you doing?

Group dynamics

Sensitivity between members of a group is important in any situation, so here are some effective ways to develop group awareness, mutual understanding and trust. Regular practice of these activities will develop cooperation, build team spirit and help the group to solve problems together.

Clap together

A quick way of establishing focus. The whole group stands in a circle with their arms outstretched, middle fingers touching. Everybody tries to clap at exactly the same time. Quite a challenge at first, it can be done with practice and concentration.

Lifting a mirror

For this game, you need a long piece of rope. Tie a knot in it and place it in a circular shape on the floor. The group stands round it and everyone gets ready to pick it up. Now imagine that it is a large circular mirror. The group's task is to pick it up together, lift it to waist height and put it down again without losing the illusion of the mirror. In other words, everyone must work together with awareness to keep the mirror level. Once they have accomplished it, they could try again, lifting it higher and perhaps tilting it, using eye contact, or under the leader's guidance.

Cross the circle

The whole group stands in a circle. One person (**A**) is chosen to start. He makes eye contact with somebody else (**B**) across the circle. When **B** becomes aware that **A** is looking at her, she says "yes" to **A**, who begins walking steadily across to take **B**'s place. As soon as **B** has said "yes", she must make eye contact with a third person (**C**). **B** must not begin walking from her place until **C** has also accepted the eye contact and said "yes". The game continues for as long as possible.

It takes a few attempts before people get the hang of it. What is paramount is that everybody pays 100% attention. Eye contact must be made very clearly. One thing that can go wrong is that **B** starts walking before she has got **C**'s attention and received a "yes". People panic because they have said "yes" and somebody is walking to take their place.

- One variation is to use people's names instead of saying "yes".
- An advanced version is to replace the "yes" with a nod.
- To make sure everybody gets a turn, ask each person to stand with their arms folded once they have crossed the circle.
- A fun version of this game is "Zombies". Whoever is crossing the circle walks slowly, holding their arms out in front like a zombie. The person they are walking towards also becomes a zombie and walks towards somebody else – as soon as they have eye contact.

Deadly handshake
A popular variation of *Wink murder*. One person is selected as the murderer by the group leader, or randomly (write "X" on one of several scraps of paper and draw lots). The game begins as people mill around the room, shaking hands with each other as though at a party. When the murderer shakes hands, he or she can kill you by tickling your palm with one finger. If the murderer tickles your hand, you must die. It is best to have a rule that people don't "die" immediately – perhaps they take five steps before dying, or shake hands with two more people, so the killer is not so easily spotted. They can die in as dramatic a fashion as they wish. At any point after the first death, a member of the group can stop the game and accuse somebody if they think they know who the murderer is. If they are wrong, the accuser also dies. If they are right, the round ends.

Energy ball
Stand in a circle and throw an imaginary ball of energy across to somebody else. As you throw, make a sound as the ball travels through the air – a different one each time.

- Eye contact is important.
- Ensure that everybody has a turn.
- Use your movement to show clearly whom you are throwing to.
- Feel the energy as you catch the ball and imagine it moving into your body until you throw.
- Try using two energy balls at once.
- Or change the shape and size of the ball each time it is thrown.
- At the beginning and if you start again, everybody can hold up their hands, wiggle their fingers and whisper "Energy, energy, energy".

Game of power

An introductory activity by Augusto Boal[1] for exploring the relationship of objects and people within the performance space. Materials required are an assortment of easily handled props, such as a small table, some chairs and a book. Invite one person to enter the space, arranging the objects to make a naturalistic or abstract scene in which one chair appears to be the most powerful object. Objects can be moved or put anywhere within the space.

This can be further developed with other students redesigning the space so that different objects seem more powerful. Next, one student enters the space and makes a frozen image, assuming a high status position. Other participants are invited to enter one by one and freeze in position, each trying to assume a higher status than everybody else in the stage picture. Discuss which strategies worked most effectively.

Human knot

The whole group forms a large circle and slowly walks toward the centre. Everyone should now try to hold hands with two other people across the circle. When there are no free hands, the leader breaks the link between any two people and the group have to carefully untangle themselves into a line - without talking. You may end up with the whole group in one line or two or more smaller groups. Believe it or knot, it works!

---

[1] For more ideas see "Games for Actors and Non-Actors" by Augusto Boal (Routledge) 1992.

Hah!

In this game, everybody tries to make the same sound and movement at exactly the same time. To begin with, one person leads the group. Everybody stands perfectly still in a circle with their arms by their sides, facing towards the centre. When the group are focussed, the leader chooses a moment to make the sound and movement as follows: she takes a small step forwards, holding both hands out towards the centre of the circle and saying "Hah!". It is a short and sharp action and sound. Everybody else has to try and anticipate when this is going to happen, so that they make the sound and action at the same time – not afterwards. Try it a few times with one person leading. After some practise, the group will start to sense when the leader is going to move. They are then ready to play the game with no leader, when the whole group has to try and sense the right moment. It is a challenging game, but can be achieved with the right degree of focus.

Noses

Walk around the space. Without letting anyone know, choose two other people in the room. Now, keep your nose exactly halfway between theirs and keep moving for as long as you can!

Touch and tell

A pair exercise for heightening sensory awareness and developing trust. Partner **A** closes her eyes. Partner **B** guides her slowly around the environment and finds five different surfaces for **A** to touch. **B** takes **A**'s hand and gently brushes her fingertips against each object. At the end, **A** opens her eyes and has to guess where and what the surfaces were.

Guess the leader

The class stands in a circle. One person (the detective) leaves the room. Somebody in the circle is chosen as the leader. She begins making a simple repeating movement which everybody else copies. The detective returns and stands in the centre of the circle. Every now and again the leader should change the movement. Everybody else changes as soon as they realise. The rest of the group should try not to look directly at the leader, so that they do not give her away. The detective tries to spot the leader and as soon as he does, the game is over and a new detective is chosen.

A good leader will be able to change the movements subtly or even quite blatantly without giving anything away through facial expression. The group as a whole can soon become proficient at playing this game – which really does help develop group awareness.

Count to 20

Sit or stand in a circle. The idea is for the group to count to twenty, one person saying one number at a time. Somebody is chosen to start the count. Anybody can say the next number - but if two or more people speak at the same time, counting must start again from the beginning. It is possible to get to twenty if everybody really concentrates - but try and be relaxed as well.

- Try doing it with and without eye contact.
- Other variations include members of the group facing outwards and closing their eyes or counting back from twenty to one.

There is only one liar

A psychological but fun group dynamics game from Augusto Boal. There should be no talking until the exercise is over. The group sits or stands in a circle and closes their eyes. The leader tells them that one person will be selected by a tap on the shoulder. The leader walks around the whole circle, then asks the group to open their eyes. The group members must look around and try to guess who was chosen. They are asked to remember who they decided upon but not to reveal it at this point.

The game is repeated. When everybody has finished looking round, the leader asks them, on the count of three, without talking, to point at the person they thought was chosen the first time. Everybody points. Now, they do the same again for the second time.

Afterwards, members are asked what it was that led them to choose a particular person, for example, the facial expression that person had. Then, on a signal, they are asked to put up their hands if they were touched the first time. They discover that no one was touched the first time. They are asked to do the same for the second time. The group discover that they were all touched the second time. There is only one liar – the workshop leader!

Trust circle

This activity depends on a high level of concentration and trust, and should only be played by adults or older children. You need a small group of between approximately six and fifteen. One person stands in the centre of a circle with everybody else standing close together around her. When everybody is focussed, the person in the centre closes her eyes. Standing as stiff as a broomstick, she begins to fall in any direction. Whoever she falls towards, catches her and pushes her back to the centre. She then continues by falling in a new direction. After a while swap over. Most people will want to try this, but nobody should be forced.

- At the beginning, don't let the person fall very far. Trust takes a while to develop and can be easily lost.
- Make it a rule that everybody is ready to catch the whole time. The entire group must take responsibility for the person in the centre.
- Put your hands out and make contact with the person before they fall very far. That way, they will trust you more and you will be ready to catch them.
- Try to always have at least two or three people catching the person together.
- You will sense when trust starts to develop and you can allow the person to fall a little further. Eventually the movement can become quite fast.
- Don't push people past the centre. Allow them to choose which new direction to fall.
- If you have a large group, you could have more than one circle, but only when the group are very experienced. The activity needs to be closely supervised.
- Some people love this game enormously, others don't. It can be a very successful way of developing a group bond.

Walk together

A great exercise for encouraging group sensitivity. Everybody finds a space in the room. On a given signal, everyone starts walking, using all the space in the room. On a second signal, everybody stops. Now, that was easy. This time, without talking, everybody must decide to start walking at the same time - and then to stop as a group at the same time. This obviously will require some practice! With sensitivity, it can be done. It is worth spending time on.

As a further challenge try this. The group spreads out into the space. One person must walk, then stop. Now - without talking - two people walk, then stop at the same time. Now three, then four, then five. If you get as far as five, you can continue the game with four, three, two then one person walking alone again. If the game goes wrong at any time, it starts again with one person walking. What usually happens is that the wrong number of people start to walk, or they don't set off or stop at the same time. Again, it is challenging, but with sensitivity, and a mutual language of complicity, it can be done. The group will be very pleased with themselves when they accomplish this!

Sailboats

The participants make a circle and imagine that they are standing around the edge of a toy boating pond. The leader stands behind one player, asks her to close her eyes and lightly pushes her so that she sets off steadily across the circle. On the other side of the "pond" the players must be ready to catch the "boat" when it arrives. The "boat" opens her eyes and takes the place of whichever person caught her. She gently pushes the person who caught her across the circle to someone else.

- Take the game slowly and remember that it always seems much further to the other side when you have your eyes closed!
- Most important is that the "boat" is gently and safely caught each time – otherwise it wouldn't be a trust game!
- As the trust develops you could try launching a second or even third boat – but hold onto them until it is safe to let them go.

Wink murder

Stand or sit in a circle. A detective is selected – and he or she leaves the room. Everyone in the circle closes their eyes. The leader walks around the outside of the circle and selects one person as the murderer by tapping them on the shoulder. The detective is invited back in the room to stand in the centre of the circle. Everybody looks around at each other – with no talking. The murderer must try to wink at one person at a time without being seen by the detective. If you are winked at, you must die. Try not to give away the identity of the murderer. People can die in as dramatic a fashion as they wish. The detective is allowed up to three guesses as to the identity of the murderer, after which the murderer must reveal him or herself. A new detective and murderer are then chosen. Warning: this game is very enjoyable! See also *Deadly handshake*.

- It is also good fun to play the game without a detective – decide on the murderer by drawing lots.

See also:

Clap the ball
Getting into groups
Grandma's footsteps
Pass the buck
Points of contact
Scene from your life
Two truths, one lie
Who am I
Yes, let's!

Concentration

As a simple focus at the beginning of a session, ask everyone to lie still, becoming aware of the in-breath and the out-breath, gradually allowing the breath to deepen.

One-two-three
A fun introductory warm-up and concentration game. In pairs, face each other. Start counting from one to three between yourselves, over and over. Now each time you or your partner says "one", that person claps their hands. Then, whenever one of you says "three", bend your knees. It's a bit like trying to pat your head and rub your stomach at the same time – in fact, you could try that afterwards!

A: "One" (Claps hands)
B: "Two"
A: "Three" (Bends knees)
B: "One" (Claps hands)
A: "Two"
B: "Three" (Bends knees)

You can also play this game in a circle:
- Count to five or six instead of three and let the group decide their own choice of actions for particular numbers before you start.
- Start counting around the circle as quickly as you can.
- If someone forgets which action they should be making on a particular number, you could give them a forfeit.
- To make it really challenging, choose an action for every number!

Clap around the circle

In a circle, each person claps in turn. Try to make it sound like one person is clapping. Now try again with your eyes closed. It's much harder!

Grandma's footsteps

The traditional children's game. One person is Grandma - she faces a wall at one end of the room. The others in the group start at the other end of the room, then try to creep up to Grandma and tap her on the shoulder. However, at any moment, Grandma can turn around suddenly. If she sees anyone moving, she points at them and that person must return to the other end of the room. Whoever manages to tap her on the shoulder becomes Grandma (male or female) and the game starts again. It's a good activity for cultivating concentration and patience - not to mention lots of cheating!

- For an "advanced" group dynamics version try playing it without Grandma!

Greetings, Your Majesty

The group stands or sits in a circle. A volunteer goes to the centre and closes their eyes or is blindfolded. The leader silently selects someone in the circle. That person must say "Greetings, your Majesty" in a disguised voice. Now the person in the middle opens their eyes and tries to guess who it was. If they are wrong, the game is played again. If they are right, they swap places.

One group of children taught me their own version of this, where the "guesser" faces the wall and the others sit behind on the floor. One person says "Fish and Chips" in a daft voice. The guesser turns round and points at who they think it was.

Keeper of the keys

The group sits in a circle. A volunteer sits in the middle and is blindfolded, with a bunch of keys placed just in front of them. Someone else is selected to creep up and try to steal the keys, returning to their place with them. Whoever is chosen must first sneak around the outside of the circle, re-entering by the space they left. If the keeper hears a sound, she points in that direction. If she points at the thief, that person returns to their place and someone else has a go. If the thief manages to take the keys and return to their place, they become the new keeper. The game encourages concentration and sensory awareness. It is important that every member of the group maintains silence. A variation is to allow more than one thief at a time. I learnt this one at cub scouts, but I still love playing it!

Pass the buck

A good way of developing alertness and group awareness. Everybody walks around the room. One person holds an easy to handle object, which is to be passed between the group members. The object may only be passed when you have eye contact with another person. The person passing the object counts out loud – each time the object is passed, the count increases from 1 to 20. If it is done well, people in the group will become very aware of one another. Once you reach that stage, a second object can be introduced. The count increases each time either of the objects is passed on. If two people count at the same time or an object is dropped, start again. This is a good warm-up for *Count to 20*.

- You can use any object, as long as it is not breakable. Try a water bottle, a book or a broomstick.
- Try throwing a ball instead of passing an object – although it is doubly important that eye contact is made before throwing, so that the ball is not dropped.

Slap, clap, click, click
Stand in a circle. The leader begins a 4/4 rhythm, which everybody joins in with:

One – slap both hands on thighs
Two – clap hands together
Three – click fingers of right hand
Four – click fingers of left hand.

Once the rhythm is established, go round the circle with everybody saying their own name on the fourth beat, as you click your fingers with your left hand. Try not to speed up.

- You can play this as a name game – on the fourth beat you say the name of the person next to you.

The next version is a little more challenging. Give a number to everybody around the circle from 1 to however many there are. Get the rhythm going again. One person begins by saying their own number on the third beat and somebody else's number on the fourth beat. Whoever's number was called on the fourth beat calls their own number on the third beat of the next bar and somebody else's number on the fourth. So it could go like this:

Slap – clap – six – ten
Slap – clap – ten– seven
Slap – clap – seven – two

And so on. If and when a mistake is made, stop the game and begin again. Emphasise the steadiness of the beat. You could have a forfeit for whoever makes a mistake – I'll leave that up to you!

Betty Botter

An effective way of focussing the group. The idea is to synchronise the chanting of a tongue twister to a rhythm and action as accurately as possible. Everybody needs to learn the following tongue twister. The underlined letters indicate the rhythm.

Betty Botter bought some butter
But she said, "This butter's bitter.
But a bit of better butter
Better than the bitter butter,
That would make my batter better."

Now get everybody doing the *slap clap click click* rhythm together. If you work it out, you can say each line of the tongue twister to the 4/4 rhythm.

slap   clap   click   click
Betty Botter bought some butter

Try to keep the rhythm constant and don't be afraid of starting again if it all goes wrong. If you get really good you could also learn the second part of the tongue twister:

So she bought some better butter
Better than the bitter butter
And it made her batter better.
So 'twas better Betty Botter
Bought a bit of better butter.

Blind walk

There are two main kinds of blind walk. The first is where one person closes their eyes and is carefully led around the room by a partner. Obviously safety is paramount. Always start slowly, remembering that it will probably seem very fast to the person who is being led. The safest way I have found is for the leader to take both the blind person's hands and walk backwards. That way, they are always watching their partner and are more able to stop them bumping into other people.

The leading partner should aim to give them a completely smooth journey, because as soon as they bump into anything, they will lose confidence. This is a great trust game – but trust has to be gained. Once it has been, you can pick up the speed a bit. With adults, if the group becomes really confident after a few sessions, you could progress onto running with your eyes closed. In this case the leader of each pair can run alongside their blind partner. Be careful!

The second version takes place outdoors, ideally in a natural setting. One partner is blindfolded and led on a sensory walk by their partner. This is an incredible way of sharpening the senses. All the same precautions apply, except that the leading partner can walk forward normally whilst still keeping an eye on their partner. The reason for this is that you have lots of space and are less likely to bump into other people. You do need to take care of uneven surfaces and give instructions to your partner about steps etc. Otherwise, try to keep talking to a minimum.

Mirror speech
In pairs, facing each other. One person starts talking about anything – very, very slowly. The other has to try and speak at the same time as their partner, without trying to lead the speech. Every now and again the teacher claps her hands for the leadership to change. It is fun to combine this with the *Mirrors* exercise. You could also try playing the game using sounds instead of words.

Desert island
A visualisation activity to encourage relaxation. Everybody finds a comfortable spot to lie on the floor. It is a good idea to dim the lights if possible. Using a soft and relaxed voice, encourage the students to imagine themselves on a desert island, along the lines of the following text. You could play some sea sound effects if you have any, or some quiet music.

Close your eyes. Let your body begin to relax. Imagine that you are lying on a deserted beach on an island in the middle of the ocean. The sun is warm, but not too hot. You can hear the surf, with waves breaking gently, one after another. The sand is soft and warm. If you like you can move your fingers slowly and feel the sand through your fingers. Stretch your body from head to toe and let go once more. As you let go of each breath, feel the tension melting away from you. A gentle breeze touches your body and rustles the branches of the nearby trees. Your feet and toes feel relaxed. Your legs feel very relaxed. You feel your breathing slow down. Slow down. Your fingers, hands and arms feel completely relaxed. You are aware of the warmth of the sun and the softness of the sand underneath you. Your whole body feels relaxed, as though it is melting into the beach. Your mind is at peace. Everything is at peace. If any thoughts come to you, you let them float away like clouds in the sky. Imagine a bird flying high in the sky above you. Now imagine you can see yourself from that bird's point of view, lying comfortably on the beach far below.

Depending on the available time, you could let the students lie in silence for several minutes.

Now you feel completely relaxed and refreshed. Become aware once more of your body lying on the beach, and the sound of the waves breaking gently on the shore. Slowly move your fingers and toes in the sand. Stretch your arms and legs. Now slowly roll over onto your right side with your knees pulled in. Take a few breaths before you come to sitting up in your own time.

See also:

Bill and Ben
Clap the ball
Clap together
Count to 20
Cross the circle
Follow the hand
Fruit salad
Group juggle
Guess the leader
Hah!
Lifting a mirror
Mirrors
Touch and Tell

Storytelling

These games will help your actors to improvise stories and story telling. It is often more interesting (and fun) to write stories through action rather than discussion.

One word stories

In a circle, the story is started, with each person in turn adding one word. It usually starts with "Once – upon – a – time...". The idea is to keep your thoughts free flowing, so that you don't try to guess what is coming or force the story in a particular direction. It is rare that the story makes a great deal of sense, although it is always amusing. If the group is too large, break into smaller groups.

- Another variation is to throw a ball around the circle in any order.
- Add your word as you throw the ball to the next person.
- This ensures that people are more attentive; although you should make sure everyone is included.

Try playing the game in pairs, where both participants act the story out as it is told. In this case, tell the story in the present tense and as "we". For example, "We – are – climbing – a – mountain. – Look – a – giant – spider– coming – towards – us. Quick – run!" You can soon create an adventure story in this way.

You can also use the one word at a time technique to create characters made up of two or more people – great fun for interview scenes!

Random images

Let your body do the thinking - this is a great exercise for tricking the mind into being creative! On your own, choose three random poses - one high up, one medium and one low down. Choose a different spot in the room for each pose. Now find a way of moving between them. Practice until you know the positions and movements off by heart.

Think of a story or situation where some or all of those movements and shapes might fit. Begin to find ways of bringing part of that story alive, through your movements from one shape to the next.

- You can be abstract or representational.
- Try adding sounds or words.
- Combine your shapes and movements with those of a partner or others in a small group to create a new story.
- This exercise is a useful way of exploring a story or theme that the group is working on.

Random sound story

Work in small groups of 4 - 6. The groups are asked to come up with a selection of random sounds - with each group member making one vocalised sound. Next, the group decides on a sequence in which these sounds are made and practices it. Each group performs its sound sequence in turn to the whole class. Now the groups are asked to make up a story in which these sounds occur - in the sequence already decided upon. The story can be narrated or acted.

Story orchestra
The whole of the group sits or stands in front of one person, who is the conductor. The conductor imagines that she is conducting an orchestra. The group tells a story, with the conductor pointing at different people in any order, one by one. The conductor decides how long each person continues to tell the story before moving on to somebody new. Of course, she may change at the end of a sentence, or at any time. The group should try to keep the narration going as smoothly as possible.

You're telling me
Partner **A** starts telling **B** what he did at the weekend. On a command from the leader, **A** continues in a whisper, then in mime, then storytelling again, then in gibberish, shouting, singing, as a particular character etc. I have often used this game in auditions.

See also:

Alphabet conversations
Breakfast serial
Scene from your life
Spin offs
Yes and...

Sound

This section covers games and activities which develop vocal awareness and an understanding of how sound may be used to create atmosphere or tell stories. Also included is 'Walking Breath' – an effective and beneficial vocal warm-up.

Beat it

A rhythmic exercise, which develops concentration and awareness. The game with all its variations can be taught over several sessions. Everybody stands in a circle. The leader gets the group to gently stamp their feet at a regular and steady beat. Other rhythms are introduced over this pulse. Begin with six sixes. Everybody counts out loud, clapping their hands on the first beat of each bar as follows:

One, two, three, four, five, six
Two, two, three, four, five, six
Three, two, three, four, five, six
Four, two, three, four, five, six
Five, two, three, four, five, six

On the last bar everybody claps on the first and last beat and then stops:

Six, two, three, four, five, **six**

Try to make sure the pulse doesn't speed up. Once the group get good at this, try it again with the stamping but without counting aloud. You can also try it with your eyes closed or with your backs to each other.

There are other patterns to learn, which also fit together. This time the group counts down from eight to one as follows:

One, two, three, four, five, six, seven, eight
One, two, three, four, five, six, seven

One, two, three, four, five, six
One, two, three, four, five
One, two, three, four
One, two, three
One, two
One

Get the whole group to learn this pattern, stopping in unison on the final "One". Then get half the group doing six sixes and the other half counting down from eight. If done properly the patterns should synchronise, with everybody clapping their hands together on the final "One". There are some nice cross-rhythms on the way.

Nine fours also fits with the other two rhythms. Practise on its own first:

One, two, three, four
Two, two, three, four
Three, two, three, four ...

And so on to:

Nine, two, three, **four.**

Rainstorm

A simple little game - with a great effect. The idea is for the whole group to create the sound of a rainstorm. They are asked to carefully follow the movements of the leader. Start by tapping one finger on the palm of your hand. It sounds just like raindrops. Slowly build the effect by using two, three, four and then five fingers so that everyone is clapping their hands really loudly.

After the storm reaches a crescendo, slowly reduce the volume with four, three, two then just one finger again tapping on the palm. You can only really appreciate this effect by trying it in a large group. I used the game in theatres to great effect in a show called "Singing in the Rainforest", where we got the whole audience playing the game!

To extend the activity after everybody is clapping their hands, you might want to progress onto slapping your thighs, followed by stamping your feet! You can also ask the group to think of words to do with a rainstorm before they start. They could whisper these, getting louder as the storm increases and then quieter again.

Sound circle

There are many games that can be played using sounds in a circle. Here are two variations. You can pass sounds around the circle: The first person makes a vocal sound. The next person copies that sound and adds another – and so on around the circle. So the first person might go: "Whoooh!". The next person could go "Whoooh! Eee-owww" and the third person "Eee-owww, Plonkety-plonk." Of course you can be a lot more imaginative with your sounds than this. It is difficult to write down really weird sounds!

The second variation is an echo: The first person makes a sound, which is echoed by the rest of the group. The second person makes a new sound that is echoed by the group and so on all the way around the circle. After that you could move onto *Sound and Action*.

Sound pictures

The leader or one member of the group acts as conductor, whilst the rest of the group are the "orchestra". Using their voices (and body percussion if appropriate!), the group paints a sound picture of a particular theme, for example the seaside, a city, a jungle. The leader controls the shape of the piece by raising her hand to increase the volume or bringing it to touch the floor for silence.

- One way to do this is to allow everybody to choose their own sound – discuss what types of sound might be appropriate before you start.
- Or, if it is a very large group, or very lively, you can divide the participants into sections, giving a particular sound for each section, then conduct them accordingly.
- You do not have to choose a theme, you could just create an abstract soundscape, with the group listening carefully to each other. You could do this lying on the floor with your eyes closed.
- The group should bear in mind contrasting and complementary sounds and try to be aware of natural peaks and troughs in the piece – or the conductor can try to create these.
- The group could try to create a sound picture for a particular mood or emotion.
- Sound pictures can easily be used as part of an improvisation or performance

Walking breath
A simple yet effective voice warm-up. Each person starts in their own space in the room. The leader gives the following directions:

Breathe out all the air in your lungs. Now take a breath. As you breathe out, start walking in any direction, watching out for other people and changing direction if you have to. Keep walking until you reach the end of the breath. Now stop and take another breath before you continue walking in a new direction. The breath should be gentle and easy. Look out to the horizon - imagine the walls aren't there.

After a couple of minutes, ask the students to introduce a low growl or hum into their voice - again not pushing the breath. Gradually, over several breaths, the voice can get a little louder. When the voice begins to warm, the hum can be opened out to a vowel sound, e.g. aaah, oooh, eeee. Students should start to tune into each other, being aware of other voices in the room.
The emphasis is on walking with the breath and being gentle with the voice until it is warm. Take your time with this exercise – warming the voice cannot be rushed.

See also:

Betty Botter
Random sound story
Sound and action

Rehearsal

Many of the preceding games will be useful as warm-ups for rehearsing a show. Here are some activities which are particularly useful during the rehearsal process. Remember, the more fun you have in rehearsals, the more creativity you and the actors will be encouraged to feed into the play.

Gibberish

Gibberish can be a useful rehearsal tool, especially when actors are not yet confident with their lines, but need to develop their movement. Take a scene and simply play it in gibberish - any nonsense sounds will do. You may find that the sounds made reflect the character or his mood in that scene. Suddenly the actors will be able to play the scene freely without having to worry about exact words. They will be forced to connect with the atmosphere, story and sub-text of the scene and will become more focussed on their own physicality and emotion.

Moulding a character

This can be played part of the way into rehearsals. One character and a line or moment from the play is chosen. The actor playing that part stands in a neutral position in front of the others. A small group are then chosen to "mould" the person into the character as they imagine him or her at that moment. No talking or discussion is allowed. The aim is to sculpt the character together until they reach a consensus. The sculptors carefully move the person's body into place. If a particular facial expression is required, it may be made by one of the sculptors and shown to the statue, who then copies it. This can be really helpful in character development and may help the actor discover new ways to physicalise the character.

Script game

A fun and challenging game to play during the latter stages of rehearsals. The actors are assembled around the acting area. The director calls out a random line from the script. Immediately the cast have to rush to where they should be at that moment (if they can remember) and start playing the scene from that line onwards. Anyone not on stage should leave or stand at the side. As soon as everyone recalls where they should be, the director stops the scene and chooses another line.

Three moments

Choose three different moments in the play for your character. Now move into a space and choose a position for your character in the first moment. Choose another space and make your second shape there. Do the same for your third moment. Now practise moving between the shapes over and over until it becomes smooth. If the leader wishes, each actor can choose a sound or a word to go with each shape. Finally half the group sits out and watches as the others go through their shapes and sounds. Then they swap so that everyone has a chance to watch. The game can teach a lot about the physicality of characters.

See also:

Cross the circle
Game of power
Pecking order
Random images
Scene from your life
Sound pictures
Status pictures

101 Drama Games and Activities

Addendum: Tongue Twisters

Here are a few tongue twisters to get your lips and teeth around. There are thousands of tongue twisters out there - these are just some of my favourites. You may also know slight variations of these - it's amazing what Chinese Whispering can do!

Remember, it's not just how fast you say them, but how clearly too.

There's a chip shop in space which sells space ship-shaped chips.

I like New York, unique New York, I like unique New York.

Two toads totally tired, tried to trot to Tewkesbury.

The Leith Police dismisseth us.

A school coal scuttle, a scuttle of school coal.

Rubber baby-buggy bouncers.

Floppy fluffy puppies, floppy fluffy puppies.

Popacatepetl, copper plated kettle.

Peggy Babcock loves Tubby Gigwhip.

She stood upon the balcony, inexplicably mimicking him hiccupping and amicably welcoming him in.

Are you copper-bottoming them my man?
No, I'm aluminiuming them ma'am.

The sixth sick sheik's sixth sheep's sick .

All I want is a proper cup of coffee,
Made in a proper copper coffee pot
I may be off my dot
But I want a cup of coffee
From a proper coffee pot.
Tin coffee pots and iron coffee pots
They're no use to me -
If I can't have a proper cup of coffee
In a proper copper coffee pot
I'll have a cup of tea.

The skunk sat on the stump. The stump thunk the skunk stunk. The skunk thunk the stump stunk. What stunk - the skunk or the stump?

What a to-do to die today at a minute or two to two,
A thing distinctly hard to say but harder still to do.
For they'll beat a tattoo at a quarter to two:
A rat-ta tat-tat ta tat-tat ta to-to.
And the dragon will come when he hears the drum
At a minute or two to two today, at a minute or two to two.
(Lewis Carroll)

Imagine an imaginary menagerie manager
Imagining managing an imaginary menagerie.

How much wood could a woodchuck chuck, if a woodchuck could chuck wood?

Toy boats, toy boats, toy boats, toy boats, toy boats.

Peter Piper picked a peck of pickled peppers
If Peter Piper picked a peck of pickled peppers
Where's the peck of pickled peppers Peter Piper picked?

Index of games

Plays by David Farmer

Frog and Toad   Based on the stories by Arnold Lobel
(Songs And Music by Robert Rigby)

Frog in Love   Based on the stories by Max Velthuijs
(Songs and Music by David Farmer)

George Speaks   Based on the book by Dick King-Smith
(Songs and Music by David Farmer)

Jack and the Beanstalk   Traditional
(Music by Kenny Forrest)

Mouse and Mole   Based on the books by Joyce Dunbar
(Songs and music by David Farmer)

My Uncle Arly   Based on the life and work of Edward Lear
(Co-written with Shôn Dale-Jones)

The Nightingale   Based on the story by Hans Christian Andersen
(Music by Kenny Forrest)

One Dark Night   Based on traditional world myths and stories
(Songs and Music by David Farmer)

Suitcase full of Stories   Based on traditional world stories

If you are interested in reading or performing any of these scripts, please contact the author at: david@david-farmer.com

Further information about the author's courses, scripts and other publications can be found at: http://www.dramaresource.com

Breinigsville, PA USA
18 August 2009
222539BV00002B/244/P

9 781847 538413